50 Iran Dishes for Home

By: Kelly Johnson

Table of Contents

- Fesenjan
- Ghormeh Sabzi
- Kebab Koobideh
- Chelow Kebab
- Zereshk Polo
- Tahchin
- Ash Reshteh
- Gheymeh
- Khoresht-e Bademjan
- Sabzi Polo
- Kebab Barg
- Kashk-e Bademjan
- Tahdig
- Shirin Polo
- Khoresht-e Gheymé
- Dizi
- Faloodeh
- Khoresh Karafs
- Kebab Joojeh
- Baghali Polo
- Khoresht-e Fesenjan
- Hummus (Iranian version)
- Dolmeh (Stuffed Grape Leaves)
- Mirza Ghasemi
- Mast-o-Khiar
- Salad Shirazi
- Kashk-e Zeytun
- Torshi
- Khoresh-e-Tamatar
- Saffron Rice Pudding (Shirin Fereni)
- Polow Ba Morgh
- Lubia Polo
- Gormeh Sabzi Kebab
- Gondi (Persian Meatball Soup)
- Ash-e-Doogh

- Eshkeneh
- Aloo Polo
- Khoresht-e-Serdari
- Dizi-e-Kabir
- Naan-o-Kabob
- Kashk-e Bademjan with Meat
- Kuku Sabzi
- Tashk-e-Morgh
- Mahi Shekam Por
- Mast-o-Musir
- Khoresht-e Albaloo
- Shirin Jow (Sweet Rice)
- Kebab Tabbah
- Baghali Ghatogh
- Saffron Rice with Raisins (Shirin Polow)

Fesenjan (Iranian Pomegranate and Walnut Stew)

Ingredients:

- 2 tbsp olive oil
- 1 lb chicken or duck, cut into pieces
- 1 large onion, finely chopped
- 2 cups walnuts, ground
- 1 cup pomegranate molasses
- 1/2 cup chicken broth
- 1 tsp turmeric
- 1 tsp cinnamon
- 1/2 tsp ground cloves
- Salt and pepper to taste
- 1 tbsp sugar (optional, for extra sweetness)

Instructions:

1. Heat olive oil in a large pot over medium heat. Brown the chicken pieces on all sides, then remove and set aside.
2. In the same pot, sauté the chopped onion until golden brown.
3. Add ground walnuts to the onions and stir for a few minutes until fragrant.
4. Add the turmeric, cinnamon, cloves, salt, pepper, and chicken broth. Stir well to combine.
5. Return the chicken to the pot, cover, and simmer on low heat for 1.5 to 2 hours, or until the chicken is tender and the sauce has thickened.
6. Stir in the pomegranate molasses and sugar (if using) and cook for an additional 15-20 minutes.
7. Serve with Persian rice (Chelow or Polo).

Ghormeh Sabzi (Persian Herb Stew)

Ingredients:

- 2 tbsp olive oil
- 1 lb lamb or beef stew meat, cut into pieces
- 1 large onion, chopped
- 4 cups fresh parsley, chopped
- 2 cups fresh cilantro, chopped
- 1/2 cup fresh fenugreek leaves (or 1 tbsp dried fenugreek)
- 1/4 cup dried Persian lime (or lime zest), pierced
- 1 tsp turmeric
- 1/2 tsp cumin
- 1/2 tsp cinnamon
- 2 cups kidney beans, cooked or canned
- Salt and pepper to taste
- 1 tbsp lemon juice (optional)

Instructions:

1. Heat olive oil in a large pot over medium heat. Brown the meat on all sides, then remove and set aside.
2. Sauté the onion in the same pot until golden, then add turmeric, cumin, and cinnamon, cooking for 1 minute.
3. Add the chopped herbs (parsley, cilantro, fenugreek) and cook, stirring frequently, until the herbs darken and soften (about 10 minutes).
4. Return the meat to the pot, add the dried lime (or lime zest), kidney beans, salt, and pepper.
5. Pour in enough water to cover the ingredients, then bring to a boil. Reduce heat to low and simmer for 2-3 hours, until the meat is tender and the flavors are well combined.
6. Stir in lemon juice (if desired) before serving. Serve with Persian rice.

Kebab Koobideh (Persian Ground Meat Kebab)

Ingredients:

- 1 lb ground lamb or beef (or a combination)
- 1 medium onion, grated
- 1/4 cup parsley, chopped
- 1 tsp turmeric
- 1 tsp sumac
- 1/2 tsp ground black pepper
- 1 tsp salt
- 2 tbsp olive oil
- 1/2 tsp saffron (optional, for extra flavor)

Instructions:

1. In a large mixing bowl, combine the ground meat, grated onion, parsley, turmeric, sumac, black pepper, and salt. Mix thoroughly, using your hands if necessary, until the mixture is smooth and cohesive.
2. Divide the meat mixture into equal portions and mold them around metal or wooden skewers.
3. Preheat the grill or broiler. Brush the kebabs with olive oil and grill on medium-high heat for 5-7 minutes per side or until cooked to your desired level of doneness.
4. If using saffron, dissolve it in a little warm water and drizzle over the cooked kebabs before serving.
5. Serve with flatbread, grilled vegetables, and rice.

Chelow Kebab (Persian Rice with Kebab)

Ingredients:

- 1 lb Kebab Koobideh or Kebab Barg (lamb, beef, or chicken)
- 2 cups basmati rice
- 2 tbsp butter
- 1/2 tsp saffron (optional, for extra flavor)
- Salt to taste

Instructions:

1. Rinse the basmati rice until the water runs clear, then soak in water for at least 30 minutes.
2. Bring a large pot of water to a boil and add the soaked rice. Cook the rice for 10-12 minutes, then drain.
3. Return the rice to the pot and add the butter. If using saffron, dissolve it in warm water and pour it over the rice. Cover the pot and cook on low heat for 15-20 minutes to allow the rice to steam.
4. Grill or broil the Kebab Koobideh or Kebab Barg according to the recipe instructions above.
5. Serve the kebabs on a bed of Chelow (Persian rice) with grilled tomatoes, sumac, and flatbread.

Zereshk Polo (Persian Barberry Rice)

Ingredients:

- 2 cups basmati rice
- 1/4 cup dried barberries (zereshk)
- 2 tbsp butter
- 1/4 cup slivered almonds or pistachios (optional)
- 1/4 tsp saffron (optional)
- 1 tbsp sugar
- Salt to taste

Instructions:

1. Rinse and soak the basmati rice for 30 minutes, then cook it in boiling salted water for 10-12 minutes. Drain the rice.
2. In a small pan, melt 1 tbsp butter and sauté the barberries for 1-2 minutes. If desired, add sugar to balance the tartness of the barberries.
3. If using saffron, dissolve it in a little warm water and pour over the rice.
4. In a large pan, melt the remaining butter and toss the rice with the barberries, saffron, and optional nuts.
5. Serve hot as a flavorful side dish or with kebabs.

Tahchin (Persian Saffron Rice Cake)

Ingredients:

- 2 cups basmati rice
- 1/2 cup yogurt
- 1/2 cup saffron-infused water
- 1 lb chicken breast (optional, cooked and shredded)
- 1 onion, sautéed
- 1/4 cup butter
- 1/2 tsp turmeric
- 1/4 cup barberries (zereshk)
- Salt to taste

Instructions:

1. Rinse and soak the basmati rice for 30 minutes. Parboil the rice until slightly soft, then drain.
2. Mix yogurt, saffron water, turmeric, and salt in a bowl. Combine with the parboiled rice.
3. Preheat the oven to 375°F (190°C). Grease a baking dish and layer the rice mixture, pressing it down firmly.
4. Add the cooked, shredded chicken and sautéed onions to the center, if using.
5. Top with butter and bake for 45-50 minutes until the top is golden and crispy.
6. Garnish with barberries and serve hot.

Ash Reshteh (Persian Noodle Soup)

Ingredients:

- 1/2 lb fresh or dried Persian noodles (reshteh)
- 1 lb lamb, beef, or chicken (optional)
- 1 large onion, chopped
- 2 cups spinach or parsley, chopped
- 1/4 cup chickpeas, cooked
- 1/4 cup kidney beans, cooked
- 1/4 cup fresh herbs (cilantro, dill, mint), chopped
- 1/4 cup dried Persian limes (optional)
- 1/2 tsp turmeric
- 1/4 tsp cinnamon
- Salt and pepper to taste
- 2 tbsp olive oil

Instructions:

1. In a large pot, sauté the onions in olive oil until golden. Add the meat (if using) and brown it with turmeric and cinnamon.
2. Add the beans, herbs, spinach, and chickpeas. Pour in enough water to cover the ingredients and simmer for 45 minutes.
3. Stir in the reshteh (noodles) and cook until soft (about 10 minutes). Add dried Persian limes if using.
4. Serve hot with a drizzle of kashk (fermented whey) and fried onions.

Gheymeh (Persian Split Pea Stew)

Ingredients:

- 1 lb beef stew meat or lamb
- 1 onion, chopped
- 1/2 cup split yellow peas
- 2 tomatoes, chopped
- 1/4 tsp cinnamon
- 1/2 tsp turmeric
- 1 tbsp tomato paste
- 2 dried Persian limes
- 1 tbsp sugar (optional)
- Salt and pepper to taste
- Fried potatoes (optional for garnish)

Instructions:

1. Brown the meat in a large pot with the chopped onion and spices (turmeric, cinnamon).
2. Add chopped tomatoes, tomato paste, and enough water to cover the mixture. Bring to a boil and simmer for 1 hour.
3. Stir in split peas, dried limes, and sugar. Simmer for another 30 minutes or until the peas are tender.
4. Garnish with fried potatoes, and serve with rice or flatbread.

Khoresht-e Bademjan (Persian Eggplant Stew)

Ingredients:

- 2 large eggplants, peeled and cut into chunks
- 1 lb beef stew meat or lamb, cut into pieces
- 1 large onion, chopped
- 3 tomatoes, chopped
- 2 tbsp tomato paste
- 1 tsp turmeric
- 1/2 tsp cinnamon
- 1/4 tsp cumin
- Salt and pepper to taste
- 1/4 cup dried lime (optional)
- 2 tbsp olive oil
- 1 cup water or beef broth
- Fresh herbs (parsley, cilantro, or mint) for garnish

Instructions:

1. In a large pot, heat olive oil over medium heat and brown the beef or lamb pieces. Remove the meat and set aside.
2. In the same pot, sauté the chopped onion until golden. Add the turmeric, cinnamon, cumin, salt, and pepper, and cook for 1 minute until fragrant.
3. Stir in the chopped tomatoes and tomato paste, cooking until the tomatoes break down and form a sauce.
4. Return the meat to the pot, add water or broth, and bring to a boil. Reduce heat, cover, and simmer for 1 to 1.5 hours, until the meat is tender.
5. While the stew is simmering, fry the eggplant chunks in a separate pan with a little oil until golden and soft.
6. Add the fried eggplants and dried lime (if using) to the stew, and cook for another 20-30 minutes.
7. Garnish with fresh herbs before serving. Serve with Persian rice (Chelow or Polo).

Sabzi Polo (Herbed Rice)

Ingredients:

- 2 cups basmati rice
- 1 bunch parsley, chopped
- 1 bunch cilantro, chopped
- 1 bunch dill, chopped
- 1/4 cup chives, chopped
- 1/4 cup scallions, chopped
- 2 tbsp butter
- 1/4 tsp saffron (optional)
- Salt to taste

Instructions:

1. Rinse and soak the rice for at least 30 minutes. Bring a large pot of salted water to a boil and add the rice. Cook for 10-12 minutes, until the rice is partially cooked. Drain the rice.
2. In a separate pot, melt butter and add the chopped herbs (parsley, cilantro, dill, chives, scallions). Sauté for 3-4 minutes until fragrant.
3. Layer the partially cooked rice and the sautéed herbs, pressing down lightly. Add saffron dissolved in a little water (if using).
4. Cover the pot with a lid and cook on low heat for 20-30 minutes to steam the rice and allow the flavors to combine.
5. Serve hot as a side dish, typically with fish or kebabs.

Kebab Barg (Persian Grilled Lamb Kebabs)

Ingredients:

- 1 lb lamb, cut into large chunks (or beef if preferred)
- 1 onion, grated
- 1/4 cup olive oil
- 1/4 cup yogurt
- 2 tbsp lemon juice
- 1 tsp turmeric
- 1 tsp sumac (optional)
- Salt and pepper to taste

Instructions:

1. In a large bowl, mix grated onion, olive oil, yogurt, lemon juice, turmeric, sumac (if using), salt, and pepper.
2. Add the lamb chunks to the marinade and mix well. Cover and refrigerate for at least 4 hours or overnight for best flavor.
3. Preheat the grill or broiler. Thread the marinated lamb onto skewers, ensuring the pieces are tightly packed.
4. Grill the kebabs over medium-high heat for 5-7 minutes on each side, or until they are cooked to your desired doneness.
5. Serve with Persian rice (Chelow), grilled vegetables, and flatbread.

Kashk-e Bademjan (Persian Eggplant Dip)

Ingredients:

- 2 large eggplants, peeled and cut into chunks
- 1 onion, chopped
- 2 garlic cloves, minced
- 1/4 cup Kashk (fermented whey)
- 1 tbsp tomato paste
- 1/2 tsp turmeric
- 1/4 tsp cinnamon
- 1/2 tsp cumin
- 1 tbsp lemon juice
- Salt and pepper to taste
- 2 tbsp olive oil
- Fresh mint, for garnish

Instructions:

1. Roast the eggplants in the oven or pan-fry them until they are soft and browned on the outside. Once cooled, mash the eggplants.
2. In a pan, heat olive oil and sauté the chopped onion and garlic until soft and golden.
3. Add turmeric, cinnamon, and cumin to the onions and cook for another 1-2 minutes.
4. Stir in the tomato paste and mashed eggplant, then cook for 10-15 minutes to allow the flavors to meld.
5. Add Kashk (fermented whey), lemon juice, salt, and pepper. Simmer for an additional 5-10 minutes, stirring occasionally.
6. Serve the dip warm, garnished with fresh mint. It is typically served with flatbread as an appetizer or side dish.

Tahdig (Persian Crispy Rice)

Ingredients:

- 2 cups basmati rice
- 2 tbsp butter
- 1/4 cup oil (vegetable or olive oil)
- 1/4 tsp saffron (optional)
- Salt to taste

Instructions:

1. Rinse the rice until the water runs clear, then soak for 30 minutes.
2. Bring a large pot of salted water to a boil, add the rice, and cook for about 10 minutes until the rice is partially cooked. Drain the rice.
3. In the same pot, melt butter and oil over medium heat. If using saffron, dissolve it in a little warm water and add it to the pot.
4. Add the partially cooked rice in layers, pressing down gently with the back of a spoon. Cover the pot with a tight-fitting lid.
5. Cook on low heat for 30-40 minutes, allowing the rice to steam and form a crispy bottom layer (Tahdig).
6. Serve the rice, flipping it onto a platter to reveal the crispy Tahdig layer.

Shirin Polo (Persian Sweet Rice)

Ingredients:

- 2 cups basmati rice
- 1/4 cup barberries (zereshk)
- 1/4 cup slivered almonds or pistachios (optional)
- 1/4 cup orange peel, chopped
- 1/4 cup butter
- 1/4 tsp saffron (optional)
- 1 tbsp sugar
- Salt to taste

Instructions:

1. Rinse and soak the basmati rice for 30 minutes, then cook it in salted water for about 10 minutes. Drain the rice.
2. In a small pan, melt 2 tbsp of butter, and sauté the barberries and orange peel for 2-3 minutes. If desired, add sugar for a sweeter flavor.
3. If using saffron, dissolve it in warm water and pour it over the rice.
4. In a large pot, melt the remaining butter and layer the partially cooked rice, pressing it down lightly. Add the sautéed barberries, orange peel, and nuts (if using).
5. Cover and steam for 20-30 minutes on low heat. Serve hot as a sweet accompaniment to savory dishes.

Khoresht-e Gheymé (Persian Split Pea Stew)

Ingredients:

- 1 lb beef stew meat or lamb, cut into pieces
- 1 large onion, chopped
- 1/2 cup split yellow peas
- 2 tomatoes, chopped
- 1 tbsp tomato paste
- 1/4 tsp cinnamon
- 1/2 tsp turmeric
- 2 dried Persian limes (optional)
- 1 tbsp sugar (optional)
- Salt and pepper to taste
- Fried potatoes (optional for garnish)

Instructions:

1. In a large pot, brown the meat with the chopped onion and spices (turmeric, cinnamon).
2. Add chopped tomatoes and tomato paste, then stir and cook for 5 minutes.
3. Add enough water to cover the mixture and bring to a boil. Reduce heat and simmer for 1-1.5 hours, until the meat is tender.
4. Stir in split peas and dried Persian limes (if using). Simmer for another 30-40 minutes.
5. Garnish with fried potatoes, and serve with rice or flatbread.

Dizi (Persian Lamb and Bean Stew)

Ingredients:

- 1 lb lamb shanks or stew meat
- 1 onion, chopped
- 1 large tomato, chopped
- 1/2 cup chickpeas, cooked
- 1/2 cup white beans, cooked
- 1 tsp turmeric
- 1/2 tsp cumin
- 1/2 tsp cinnamon
- 1/4 tsp black pepper
- 2 dried Persian limes
- Salt to taste
- 1-2 tbsp olive oil

Instructions:

1. In a large pot, heat olive oil and brown the lamb with the chopped onion.
2. Add turmeric, cumin, cinnamon, and black pepper. Stir for 1-2 minutes until fragrant.
3. Add chopped tomatoes, chickpeas, beans, and enough water to cover the ingredients. Bring to a boil, reduce the heat, and simmer for 1.5-2 hours until the meat is tender.
4. Add dried Persian limes and salt to taste.
5. Serve with flatbread, and enjoy with a side of fresh herbs.

Faloodeh (Persian Frozen Dessert)

Ingredients:

- 2 cups rose water
- 1 cup sugar
- 1/4 cup cornstarch
- 1/2 cup vermicelli noodles (thin rice noodles)
- 1 tbsp lemon juice (optional)
- Crushed ice for serving
- Pistachios or ground cinnamon for garnish (optional)

Instructions:

1. In a saucepan, combine rose water and sugar. Bring to a simmer and stir until the sugar is dissolved, then set aside to cool.
2. In a separate pot, bring 4 cups of water to a boil. Add the vermicelli noodles and cook until they are soft, about 3-5 minutes. Drain and rinse with cold water.
3. Dissolve the cornstarch in a small amount of cold water, then add it to the rose water syrup. Heat the mixture over low heat, stirring constantly until it thickens slightly.
4. Once the syrup is cooled, mix it with the cooked noodles. Place the mixture in a shallow pan or tray and freeze for several hours or overnight.
5. Before serving, scrape the frozen mixture with a fork to create a slushy, crystalline texture. Serve in bowls, topped with crushed ice and optionally garnish with pistachios or ground cinnamon.

Khoresh Karafs (Persian Celery Stew)

Ingredients:

- 1 lb beef or lamb stew meat, cut into pieces
- 2 onions, chopped
- 1 bunch celery, cut into small pieces
- 1/2 cup parsley, chopped
- 1/4 cup cilantro, chopped
- 1/4 cup dill, chopped
- 1 tsp turmeric
- 1/2 tsp cinnamon
- 1/2 tsp black pepper
- 2 tbsp tomato paste
- 1/4 cup lemon juice or dried lime powder
- Salt to taste
- 2 tbsp olive oil

Instructions:

1. In a pot, heat olive oil and sauté the chopped onions until golden.
2. Add turmeric, cinnamon, black pepper, and salt. Stir for 1-2 minutes until fragrant.
3. Add the stew meat to the pot and brown on all sides. Stir in tomato paste and cook for another 2-3 minutes.
4. Add water to cover the meat and bring to a boil. Reduce heat and simmer for 1 hour until the meat is tender.
5. Add the chopped celery and fresh herbs (parsley, cilantro, dill). Continue cooking for another 30 minutes to an hour.
6. Stir in lemon juice or dried lime powder for a tangy flavor, adjust seasoning, and serve with rice.

Kebab Joojeh (Persian Chicken Kebab)

Ingredients:

- 4 chicken breasts or thighs, cut into chunks
- 1 large onion, grated
- 1/4 cup plain yogurt
- 1/4 cup lemon juice
- 2 tbsp olive oil
- 1/2 tsp turmeric
- 1/2 tsp saffron (optional)
- 1/4 tsp cumin
- Salt and pepper to taste

Instructions:

1. In a bowl, combine grated onion, yogurt, lemon juice, olive oil, turmeric, saffron (if using), cumin, salt, and pepper.
2. Add the chicken chunks to the marinade and mix to coat evenly. Cover and refrigerate for at least 4 hours or overnight.
3. Preheat the grill or broiler. Thread the marinated chicken onto skewers.
4. Grill the kebabs over medium heat, turning occasionally, for about 10-12 minutes or until the chicken is cooked through.
5. Serve with rice, grilled vegetables, or flatbread.

Baghali Polo (Persian Rice with Dill and Fava Beans)

Ingredients:

- 2 cups basmati rice
- 1/2 cup fava beans (or lima beans)
- 1/2 cup fresh dill, chopped
- 1/4 cup saffron water (optional)
- 2 tbsp butter
- Salt to taste

Instructions:

1. Soak the rice for 30 minutes. Bring a large pot of salted water to a boil, then add the rice and cook for 10-12 minutes, until partially cooked. Drain and set aside.
2. In another pot, cook the fava beans in water until tender. Drain them.
3. In a large pot, layer the cooked rice, fava beans, and chopped dill. Drizzle with saffron water (if using).
4. Cover with a lid and steam on low heat for 20-30 minutes, until the rice is fully cooked.
5. Serve hot with a side of kebabs or stews.

Khoresht-e Fesenjan (Persian Pomegranate and Walnut Stew)

Ingredients:

- 1 lb chicken, duck, or beef (cut into pieces)
- 2 large onions, finely chopped
- 1 1/2 cups walnuts, ground
- 1 cup pomegranate molasses or fresh pomegranate juice
- 1/2 tsp turmeric
- 1/2 tsp cinnamon
- 1 tbsp sugar (optional)
- Salt and pepper to taste
- 2 tbsp olive oil

Instructions:

1. In a large pot, heat olive oil and sauté the onions until golden.
2. Add turmeric and cinnamon, then stir in the meat pieces, browning them on all sides.
3. Add ground walnuts and cook for another 5 minutes, stirring constantly.
4. Stir in pomegranate molasses or juice, sugar, salt, and pepper, then add enough water to cover the meat. Bring to a boil.
5. Reduce heat, cover, and simmer for 1.5-2 hours until the meat is tender and the sauce has thickened.
6. Serve with Persian rice (Chelow or Polo).

Hummus (Iranian Version)

Ingredients:

- 1 can (15 oz) chickpeas, drained and rinsed
- 2 tbsp tahini
- 2 tbsp olive oil
- 2 tbsp lemon juice
- 1 garlic clove, minced
- 1/2 tsp cumin
- Salt to taste
- Water to adjust consistency

Instructions:

1. In a food processor, combine chickpeas, tahini, olive oil, lemon juice, garlic, cumin, and salt. Process until smooth.
2. Add water, one tablespoon at a time, to achieve the desired consistency.
3. Transfer to a serving bowl, drizzle with olive oil, and garnish with parsley or paprika. Serve with flatbread or vegetables.

Dolmeh (Stuffed Grape Leaves)

Ingredients:

- 1 jar grape leaves, drained and rinsed
- 1 cup rice, rinsed
- 1/2 lb ground beef or lamb
- 1 onion, chopped
- 1/4 cup dried cranberries or currants
- 1/4 cup pine nuts
- 1/2 tsp cinnamon
- 1 tsp turmeric
- Salt and pepper to taste
- 2 tbsp olive oil
- 1 tbsp lemon juice

Instructions:

1. In a pan, sauté onions with olive oil until soft. Add the ground meat and brown. Stir in the rice, dried cranberries or currants, pine nuts, cinnamon, turmeric, salt, and pepper.
2. Place grape leaves on a flat surface, shiny side down. Place a spoonful of the filling near the base of each leaf and fold in the sides, then roll tightly.
3. Arrange the stuffed grape leaves in a pot, layering them tightly. Pour water over the top, cover, and simmer for about 1 hour, or until the rice is fully cooked.
4. Drizzle with lemon juice before serving.

Mirza Ghasemi (Persian Smoked Eggplant and Tomato Dish)

Ingredients:

- 2 large eggplants
- 2 tomatoes, chopped
- 3 garlic cloves, minced
- 1/2 tsp turmeric
- 1/4 tsp cumin
- 2 tbsp olive oil
- Salt and pepper to taste
- Fresh parsley for garnish

Instructions:

1. Roast the eggplants over an open flame or in the oven until the skin is charred. Peel off the skin and mash the flesh.
2. In a pan, heat olive oil and sauté the garlic until golden. Add the chopped tomatoes, turmeric, cumin, salt, and pepper. Cook until the tomatoes break down into a sauce.
3. Stir in the mashed eggplant and cook for another 10-15 minutes to allow the flavors to meld.
4. Garnish with fresh parsley and serve with flatbread or rice.

Mast-o-Khiar (Persian Yogurt and Cucumber Dip)

Ingredients:

- 2 cups plain yogurt (preferably whole-fat)
- 1 cucumber, finely grated or chopped
- 1 garlic clove, minced
- 2 tbsp fresh dill, chopped (or dried if fresh is unavailable)
- 1 tbsp dried mint
- 1 tbsp olive oil
- 1/2 tsp salt
- 1/4 tsp black pepper

Instructions:

1. In a bowl, combine yogurt, grated cucumber, garlic, dill, mint, olive oil, salt, and pepper.
2. Stir well until all ingredients are thoroughly mixed.
3. Chill the yogurt mixture for at least 30 minutes in the refrigerator to allow the flavors to meld.
4. Serve chilled as a side dish or appetizer with flatbread or vegetables.

Salad Shirazi (Persian Cucumber and Tomato Salad)

Ingredients:

- 2 cucumbers, peeled and diced
- 2 tomatoes, diced
- 1/2 red onion, finely chopped
- 1/4 cup fresh parsley, chopped
- 2 tbsp fresh mint, chopped
- 2 tbsp lemon juice
- 2 tbsp olive oil
- Salt and pepper to taste

Instructions:

1. In a large bowl, combine the cucumbers, tomatoes, red onion, parsley, and mint.
2. Drizzle the salad with lemon juice and olive oil, then season with salt and pepper to taste.
3. Toss everything together and chill for at least 15-20 minutes before serving to enhance the flavors.
4. Serve as a refreshing side dish with Persian stews and grilled meats.

Kashk-e Zeytun (Persian Eggplant and Yogurt Dip)

Ingredients:

- 2 large eggplants, peeled and chopped
- 1 onion, chopped
- 3 garlic cloves, minced
- 1/4 cup kashk (fermented whey) or substitute with thick yogurt
- 1 tbsp olive oil
- 1/2 tsp turmeric
- 1/2 tsp cumin
- 1/2 tsp dried mint
- 1/4 tsp chili flakes (optional)
- Salt and pepper to taste
- Fresh parsley for garnish

Instructions:

1. Roast or grill the eggplants until the skin is charred and the flesh becomes tender. Peel off the skin and mash the flesh.
2. In a pan, heat olive oil and sauté the chopped onion and garlic until softened.
3. Add turmeric, cumin, mint, and chili flakes (if using), and cook for another 2 minutes.
4. Stir in the mashed eggplant and kashk (or yogurt). Cook for about 10-15 minutes, stirring occasionally.
5. Season with salt and pepper to taste. Garnish with fresh parsley before serving.
6. Serve as a dip with flatbread or as part of a Persian meal.

Torshi (Persian Pickles)

Ingredients:

- 2 cups mixed vegetables (carrots, cauliflower, cucumbers, green beans, etc.)
- 1 cup white vinegar
- 1/2 cup water
- 1/4 cup salt
- 2 cloves garlic, crushed
- 1 tbsp turmeric
- 1 tbsp coriander seeds
- 1 tbsp dill seeds
- 1 tsp black peppercorns
- 2 tbsp sugar

Instructions:

1. Clean and chop the vegetables into small pieces or chunks.
2. In a large jar or container, layer the vegetables with garlic, turmeric, coriander seeds, dill seeds, and peppercorns.
3. In a saucepan, bring the vinegar, water, salt, and sugar to a boil. Stir until the sugar and salt dissolve.
4. Pour the hot brine over the vegetables, ensuring they are fully submerged.
5. Seal the jar and let it sit for at least a week in a cool, dark place for the flavors to develop.
6. Serve as a tangy side dish to Persian meals.

Khoresh-e-Tamatar (Persian Tomato Stew)

Ingredients:

- 2 lbs beef stew meat or lamb, cut into pieces
- 3 large tomatoes, chopped
- 1 large onion, chopped
- 2 garlic cloves, minced
- 1 tsp turmeric
- 1 tsp ground cumin
- 2 tbsp tomato paste
- 1/2 cup water or beef broth
- Salt and pepper to taste
- Olive oil for cooking

Instructions:

1. In a pot, heat olive oil and sauté the chopped onion until golden.
2. Add the minced garlic and spices (turmeric and cumin), cooking for 1-2 minutes until fragrant.
3. Stir in the meat and brown on all sides. Add tomato paste and chopped tomatoes, stirring to combine.
4. Add water or broth, cover, and simmer for 1-1.5 hours, or until the meat is tender.
5. Season with salt and pepper to taste.
6. Serve with steamed rice.

Saffron Rice Pudding (Shirin Fereni)

Ingredients:

- 1 cup rice (preferably short-grain)
- 4 cups milk
- 1/2 cup sugar
- 1/4 tsp saffron, dissolved in 2 tbsp hot water
- 1 tbsp rose water (optional)
- Chopped pistachios and almonds for garnish
- Ground cinnamon for garnish

Instructions:

1. Rinse the rice and cook it in a pot with water until soft.
2. In a separate pan, heat the milk and sugar over medium heat, stirring occasionally until it starts to thicken.
3. Add the cooked rice to the milk mixture and cook on low heat, stirring constantly.
4. Once the rice pudding thickens, stir in the saffron water and rose water.
5. Pour the pudding into serving bowls and chill for several hours.
6. Garnish with pistachios, almonds, and cinnamon before serving.

Polow Ba Morgh (Persian Rice with Chicken)

Ingredients:

- 2 cups basmati rice, soaked for 30 minutes
- 4 chicken thighs or drumsticks
- 1 large onion, sliced
- 1/4 tsp turmeric
- 1/2 tsp cinnamon
- 1/4 tsp black pepper
- 1/4 cup dried barberries (zereshk), soaked
- 1/4 cup saffron water (optional)
- 2 tbsp olive oil
- Salt to taste

Instructions:

1. In a pot, heat olive oil and sauté the onions until golden.
2. Add the chicken, turmeric, cinnamon, pepper, and salt. Brown the chicken on all sides.
3. Add enough water to cover the chicken, bring to a boil, then reduce to simmer for 45 minutes or until the chicken is cooked through.
4. In another pot, cook the soaked rice in salted water until tender, then drain.
5. In a large pot, layer the rice and chicken. Drizzle with saffron water and top with barberries.
6. Steam the rice on low heat for 20-30 minutes.
7. Serve with a side of yogurt or salad.

Lubia Polo (Persian Rice with Green Beans and Meat)

Ingredients:

- 2 cups basmati rice, soaked
- 1 lb beef or lamb stew meat, cut into pieces
- 1 large onion, chopped
- 2 garlic cloves, minced
- 1 cup green beans, chopped
- 1 tsp turmeric
- 1/2 tsp cumin
- 2 tbsp tomato paste
- Salt and pepper to taste
- Olive oil for cooking

Instructions:

1. In a pan, sauté onions and garlic in olive oil until golden.
2. Add the meat and brown it on all sides. Stir in turmeric, cumin, and tomato paste. Cook for 2-3 minutes.
3. Add water to cover the meat, bring to a boil, and simmer for 1 hour or until tender.
4. Meanwhile, blanch the green beans in boiling water for 5 minutes, then drain.
5. Cook the soaked rice until tender, then drain.
6. In a pot, layer the rice, meat mixture, and green beans. Steam for 20-30 minutes on low heat.
7. Serve with yogurt or a salad.

Gormeh Sabzi Kebab (Persian Herb Stew with Kebab)

Ingredients for Gormeh Sabzi:

- 1 lb beef stew meat or lamb, cut into pieces
- 1 onion, chopped
- 1 bunch parsley, chopped
- 1 bunch cilantro, chopped
- 1 bunch green onions, chopped
- 1/2 tsp turmeric
- 1/4 tsp dried lime powder (or substitute with lemon juice)
- Salt and pepper to taste
- 2 tbsp olive oil

Ingredients for Kebab:

- 1 lb ground lamb or beef
- 1 onion, grated
- 1/4 tsp cumin
- Salt and pepper to taste

Instructions for Gormeh Sabzi:

1. Sauté the chopped onions in olive oil until golden. Add turmeric and sauté for 1-2 minutes.
2. Add the stew meat and brown on all sides. Stir in the herbs and dried lime powder.
3. Add water to cover the meat and simmer for 1.5-2 hours until tender. Season with salt and pepper to taste.

Instructions for Kebab:

1. Mix the ground meat with grated onion, cumin, salt, and pepper.
2. Shape the mixture into kebab skewers and grill or cook on a stovetop grill until browned.
3. Serve the kebabs with the Gormeh Sabzi stew and rice.

Gondi (Persian Meatball Soup)

Ingredients:

- 1 lb ground chicken or beef
- 1/2 cup chickpea flour
- 1/4 cup rice, soaked
- 1 onion, grated
- 1 egg
- 1/2 tsp turmeric
- 1/2 tsp ground cinnamon
- 1/4 tsp black pepper
- 1/2 tsp salt
- 1/4 cup fresh parsley, chopped
- 1/4 cup fresh cilantro, chopped
- 4 cups chicken or beef broth
- 1/4 cup dried yellow split peas (optional)

Instructions:

1. In a large bowl, mix the ground meat, chickpea flour, soaked rice, grated onion, egg, turmeric, cinnamon, salt, and pepper. Add fresh parsley and cilantro and knead the mixture until it comes together.
2. Form the mixture into small meatballs, about 1-inch in diameter.
3. In a large pot, bring the broth to a boil. Carefully add the meatballs and dried split peas (if using) to the pot.
4. Lower the heat to a simmer, and cook for about 1-1.5 hours, until the meatballs are cooked through.
5. Serve hot with a side of bread.

Ash-e-Doogh (Persian Yogurt Soup)

Ingredients:

- 2 cups plain yogurt
- 1/2 cup dried herbs (mint, basil, tarragon)
- 1/2 cup rice, soaked
- 1/2 cup chickpeas, soaked overnight
- 1 onion, chopped
- 2 garlic cloves, minced
- 4 cups vegetable or chicken broth
- 1/2 tsp turmeric
- Salt and pepper to taste
- 2 tbsp olive oil
- 1 tbsp dried mint for garnish

Instructions:

1. In a pot, heat olive oil and sauté the onion and garlic until soft and fragrant.
2. Add the turmeric and dried herbs, and stir for a minute.
3. Add the soaked rice, chickpeas, and broth. Bring to a boil, then simmer for about 40 minutes, until the chickpeas are tender.
4. In a bowl, whisk together the yogurt with a bit of the hot broth to temper it, then slowly add it to the soup, stirring constantly.
5. Simmer for another 10-15 minutes, then season with salt and pepper.
6. Garnish with dried mint and serve hot.

Eshkeneh (Persian Onion Soup)

Ingredients:

- 4 large onions, thinly sliced
- 1 tbsp olive oil
- 1 tsp turmeric
- 1/2 tsp cumin
- 4 cups chicken or vegetable broth
- 1/2 cup chickpea flour
- 1 egg (optional)
- Salt and pepper to taste
- Fresh parsley for garnish

Instructions:

1. In a large pot, heat olive oil over medium heat. Add the onions and sauté until golden brown, about 15-20 minutes.
2. Add turmeric and cumin, stirring to coat the onions.
3. Pour in the broth, and bring to a boil. Reduce the heat and simmer for 20 minutes.
4. In a separate bowl, mix the chickpea flour with a little water to form a smooth paste.
5. Stir the chickpea flour mixture into the soup and simmer for an additional 10-15 minutes until the soup thickens.
6. If using, whisk the egg and drizzle it into the soup while stirring to create silky strands of egg.
7. Season with salt and pepper to taste and garnish with fresh parsley before serving.

Aloo Polo (Persian Rice with Potatoes)

Ingredients:

- 2 cups basmati rice, soaked
- 2 large potatoes, peeled and sliced
- 1 onion, chopped
- 2 tbsp vegetable oil
- 1/2 tsp turmeric
- 1/2 tsp cinnamon
- Salt and pepper to taste
- 4 tbsp fresh cilantro, chopped
- 1/4 cup saffron water (optional)

Instructions:

1. In a pan, heat the oil and sauté the onions until golden brown. Add the turmeric and cinnamon, cooking for another 2 minutes.
2. Add the rice to the pot and stir to coat it with the spices. Pour in 4 cups of water and add salt to taste. Cook the rice until it is about halfway done (firm but tender).
3. Meanwhile, heat vegetable oil in a pan and fry the potato slices until golden brown.
4. Layer the rice with the fried potatoes in a large pot, creating alternating layers. Pour the saffron water over the top (if using).
5. Cover and cook the rice over low heat for about 20-25 minutes to steam and develop a crispy bottom (tahdig).
6. Serve the rice with a side of yogurt and fresh cilantro.

Khoresht-e-Serdari (Persian Stew with Lamb and Vegetables)

Ingredients:

- 1 lb lamb, cut into chunks
- 1 onion, chopped
- 2 tomatoes, chopped
- 1 tbsp tomato paste
- 1/2 tsp turmeric
- 1/2 tsp ground cinnamon
- 1/2 cup fresh parsley, chopped
- 1/2 cup fresh cilantro, chopped
- 1/2 tsp dried lime powder (optional)
- Salt and pepper to taste
- 4 cups beef or chicken broth

Instructions:

1. In a pot, sauté the chopped onion in olive oil until softened. Add the lamb and brown it on all sides.
2. Stir in the turmeric, cinnamon, and tomato paste. Cook for 1-2 minutes to toast the spices.
3. Add the chopped tomatoes, fresh herbs, and broth. Bring to a boil, then reduce to a simmer.
4. Cover and cook for 1.5-2 hours, or until the lamb is tender and the flavors meld together.
5. Season with dried lime powder (if using), salt, and pepper to taste. Serve with steamed rice.

Dizi-e-Kabir (Traditional Persian Stew with Lamb and Beans)

Ingredients:

- 1 lb lamb (with bones)
- 2 large potatoes, peeled and cubed
- 2 cups dried yellow split peas
- 2 tomatoes, chopped
- 1 onion, chopped
- 1/2 tsp turmeric
- 1/2 tsp cumin
- 4 cups beef broth
- Salt and pepper to taste

Instructions:

1. In a large pot, sauté the onion in oil until golden brown. Add the lamb and brown on all sides.
2. Stir in turmeric and cumin, and cook for 1-2 minutes.
3. Add the potatoes, tomatoes, split peas, and broth. Bring to a boil, then reduce to a simmer.
4. Cover and cook for 1.5-2 hours, until the lamb is tender and the peas are cooked.
5. Season with salt and pepper to taste.
6. Serve the stew with flatbread and enjoy dipping the meat into the broth.

Naan-o-Kabob (Persian Kebab with Flatbread)

Ingredients:

- 1 lb ground beef or lamb
- 1 onion, grated
- 1 tsp turmeric
- 1 tsp cumin
- 1/2 tsp cinnamon
- 1/2 tsp black pepper
- Salt to taste
- Flatbreads (lavash or pita) for serving
- Fresh herbs (parsley, mint) for garnish

Instructions:

1. Mix the ground meat, grated onion, spices, and salt in a bowl. Knead the mixture until it becomes smooth and cohesive.
2. Shape the mixture into long kebab skewers or patties.
3. Grill the kebabs on a barbecue or cook them in a skillet over medium-high heat, turning occasionally until browned and cooked through.
4. Serve with flatbread and fresh herbs.

Kashk-e Bademjan with Meat (Persian Eggplant Dip with Meat)

Ingredients:

- 2 large eggplants, roasted and mashed
- 1 lb ground beef or lamb
- 1 onion, chopped
- 2 garlic cloves, minced
- 1 tbsp tomato paste
- 1/2 tsp turmeric
- 1/2 tsp cumin
- 1/2 tsp ground coriander
- 1/4 cup kashk (fermented whey) or thick yogurt
- Salt and pepper to taste
- Fresh parsley for garnish

Instructions:

1. In a pan, sauté the onion and garlic until golden. Add the ground meat and cook until browned.
2. Stir in the spices and tomato paste, cooking for 2-3 minutes.
3. Add the roasted, mashed eggplant to the pan and mix well. Stir in the kashk (or yogurt) and cook for another 10 minutes.
4. Season with salt and pepper to taste.
5. Serve as a dip or side dish, garnished with fresh parsley.

Kuku Sabzi (Persian Herb Frittata)

Ingredients:

- 6 eggs
- 2 cups fresh parsley, chopped
- 1 cup fresh cilantro, chopped
- 1/4 cup fresh dill, chopped
- 1/2 onion, finely chopped
- 1/4 tsp turmeric
- 1/4 tsp ground black pepper
- Salt to taste
- Olive oil for frying

Instructions:

1. In a bowl, whisk the eggs and mix in the fresh herbs, onion, turmeric, pepper, and salt.
2. Heat olive oil in a large pan over medium heat. Pour the egg mixture into the pan.
3. Cook for about 5-7 minutes on one side, then flip the kuku over (using a plate to help) and cook for another 5 minutes on the other side.
4. Serve warm, garnished with additional herbs or yogurt.

Tashk-e-Morgh (Persian Stew with Chicken and Walnuts)

Ingredients:

- 1 lb chicken (cut into pieces)
- 1 onion, chopped
- 2 cloves garlic, minced
- 1/2 cup ground walnuts
- 1/2 tsp turmeric
- 1/2 tsp cinnamon
- 1/4 tsp saffron threads, soaked in warm water
- 1/4 cup pomegranate molasses
- 2 tbsp tomato paste
- 3 cups chicken broth
- Salt and pepper to taste
- Fresh parsley for garnish

Instructions:

1. In a large pot, sauté the chopped onion and garlic in oil until golden.
2. Add the chicken pieces and brown them on all sides.
3. Stir in the turmeric, cinnamon, and tomato paste, cooking for a few minutes.
4. Add the ground walnuts, saffron water, pomegranate molasses, and chicken broth to the pot. Bring to a boil, then reduce the heat and simmer for 40-45 minutes until the chicken is cooked through and the sauce thickens.
5. Season with salt and pepper to taste. Garnish with fresh parsley and serve with rice.

Mahi Shekam Por (Stuffed Fish)

Ingredients:

- 2 whole fish (such as trout or sea bass), cleaned and gutted
- 1 onion, chopped
- 1/4 cup fresh herbs (parsley, dill, cilantro)
- 1/4 cup walnuts, chopped
- 2 cloves garlic, minced
- 1 tsp turmeric
- 1 tsp cumin
- 1/4 tsp cinnamon
- 1/2 lemon, juiced
- 2 tbsp olive oil
- Salt and pepper to taste

Instructions:

1. In a bowl, mix the chopped onion, garlic, fresh herbs, walnuts, turmeric, cumin, cinnamon, lemon juice, and a pinch of salt and pepper.
2. Stuff the fish with the prepared mixture, securing the opening with kitchen string or toothpicks.
3. Heat olive oil in a pan over medium heat. Place the stuffed fish in the pan and cook for about 5-7 minutes on each side, until the fish is browned and cooked through.
4. Serve the stuffed fish with a side of saffron rice.

Mast-o-Musir (Yogurt with Shallots)

Ingredients:

- 1 cup plain yogurt
- 1/4 cup dried shallots (musir), soaked in warm water for 15 minutes
- 1 tbsp olive oil
- 1/4 tsp turmeric
- Salt to taste
- Fresh mint for garnish

Instructions:

1. In a bowl, combine the yogurt, soaked shallots, olive oil, and turmeric. Stir to combine.
2. Season with salt to taste.
3. Garnish with fresh mint before serving as a side dish or appetizer.

Khoresht-e-Albaloo (Persian Sour Cherry Stew)

Ingredients:

- 1 lb lamb or beef, cut into chunks
- 2 cups sour cherries, pitted (fresh or frozen)
- 1 onion, chopped
- 2 cloves garlic, minced
- 1 tbsp tomato paste
- 1/2 tsp turmeric
- 1/2 tsp cinnamon
- 1 tbsp sugar
- 2 tbsp pomegranate molasses
- 4 cups beef or chicken broth
- Salt and pepper to taste

Instructions:

1. In a large pot, sauté the chopped onion and garlic in oil until golden.
2. Add the meat and brown it on all sides.
3. Stir in the turmeric, cinnamon, and tomato paste, cooking for a couple of minutes.
4. Add the sour cherries, sugar, pomegranate molasses, and broth to the pot. Bring to a boil, then reduce to a simmer.
5. Cook for about 1.5 hours, or until the meat is tender and the sauce thickens.
6. Season with salt and pepper to taste, and serve with rice.

Shirin Jow (Sweet Rice)

Ingredients:

- 1 1/2 cups basmati rice
- 1/2 cup sugar
- 1/4 cup saffron water
- 1/2 cup almonds, slivered
- 1/2 cup pistachios, chopped
- 1/2 cup dried barberries (zante currants)
- 1/4 cup orange blossom water (optional)
- 2 tbsp butter
- Salt to taste

Instructions:

1. Wash and soak the rice for 30 minutes. Then, cook the rice in boiling salted water until tender but firm.
2. In a pan, melt the butter and sauté the almonds, pistachios, and dried barberries for 2-3 minutes.
3. Add the sugar and saffron water to the pan, stirring until the sugar dissolves.
4. Mix the cooked rice with the nuts, barberries, and saffron mixture, ensuring even coating.
5. Add the orange blossom water (if using) and gently fold it into the rice.
6. Serve warm as a sweet side dish.

Kebab Tabbah (Pan-Fried Kebab)

Ingredients:

- 1 lb ground lamb or beef
- 1 onion, grated
- 2 cloves garlic, minced
- 1/2 tsp turmeric
- 1/2 tsp cumin
- 1/4 tsp cinnamon
- Salt and pepper to taste
- Olive oil for frying

Instructions:

1. In a bowl, combine the ground meat, grated onion, garlic, spices, salt, and pepper. Knead until smooth.
2. Form the mixture into small patties or logs.
3. Heat olive oil in a skillet over medium-high heat. Fry the kebabs, turning occasionally, until browned on all sides and cooked through (about 8-10 minutes).
4. Serve with flatbread, grilled vegetables, and a side of yogurt.

Baghali Ghatogh (Persian Fava Bean Stew)

Ingredients:

- 2 cups fresh or frozen fava beans (baghali)
- 1 onion, chopped
- 3 cloves garlic, minced
- 1/2 tsp turmeric
- 1/2 tsp cumin
- 1/2 tsp ground coriander
- 2 tbsp fresh dill, chopped
- 2 tbsp olive oil
- 1/2 cup water or broth
- Salt and pepper to taste
- 2 eggs (optional)

Instructions:

1. In a pan, sauté the onion and garlic in olive oil until softened.
2. Stir in the turmeric, cumin, and ground coriander, cooking for 1-2 minutes.
3. Add the fava beans and water or broth. Cook for 15-20 minutes, until the beans are tender.
4. Stir in the fresh dill and season with salt and pepper.
5. Optionally, crack two eggs into the stew and stir until they are cooked into the sauce.
6. Serve with rice.

Saffron Rice with Raisins (Shirin Polow)

Ingredients:

- 2 cups basmati rice
- 1/2 cup raisins
- 1/4 cup slivered almonds
- 1/4 cup pistachios, chopped
- 1/4 cup saffron water
- 2 tbsp sugar
- 2 tbsp butter
- Salt to taste

Instructions:

1. Wash and soak the rice for 30 minutes. Cook the rice in boiling salted water until tender but firm.
2. In a pan, melt the butter and sauté the raisins, almonds, and pistachios for 2-3 minutes.
3. Add the saffron water and sugar, stirring until the sugar dissolves.
4. Gently fold the sweet mixture into the cooked rice.
5. Serve as a fragrant, sweet accompaniment to meat dishes.

www.ingramcontent.com/pod-product-compliance
Lightning Source LLC
LaVergne TN
LVHW081339060526
838201LV00055B/2750